INDIAN RHINOCEROSES

Bethany Baxter

PowerKiDS press
New York

Published in 2014 by The Rosen Publishing Group, Inc.
29 East 21st Street, New York, NY 10010

First Edition

Editor: Julia Quinlan
Book Design: Greg Tucker

Photo Credits: Cover neelsky/Shutterstock.com; p. 4 Nelik/Shutterstock.com; p. 5 Nataiki/Shutterstock.com; p. 6 Jeremy Richards/Shutterstock.com; p. 7 Stephen/Shutterstock.com; p. 8 James Warwick/Stone/Getty Images; pp. 9, 16, 18 Steve Winter/National Geographic/Getty Images; p. 10 Cordier Sylvain/hemis.fr/Getty Images; pp. 10–11 © iStockphoto.com/Carsten Brandt; p. 11 Gelia/Shutterstock.com; pp. 12–13 Visuals Unlimited, Inc./Gerard Lacz/Getty Images; p. 14 wildlywise/Shutterstock.com; p. 15 Bart Acke/Shutterstock.com; p. 17 Alan Jeffery/Getty Images; p. 19 Eduard Kyslynskyy/Shutterstock.com; p. 21 Stockbyte/Getty Images; p. 22 Reto Puppetti/Picture Press/Getty Images.

Library of Congress Cataloging-in-Publication Data

Baxter, Bethany.
 Indian rhinoceroses / by Bethany Baxter. — 1st ed.
    p. cm. — (Awesome armored animals)
 Includes index.
 ISBN 978-1-4777-0794-4 (library binding) — ISBN 978-1-4777-0960-3 (pbk.) — ISBN 978-1-4777-0961-0 (6-pack)
 1. Indian rhinoceros—Juvenile literature. 2. Indian rhinoceros—Conservation—Juvenile literature. I. Title.
 QL737.U63B39 2014
 599.66'8—dc23
                        2012048580

Manufactured in the United States of America

CPSIA Compliance Information: Batch #S13PK6: For Further Information contact Rosen Publishing, New York, New York at 1-800-237-9932

Contents

Just One Horn!

Indian rhinoceroses are large plant-eating animals. They are **native** to southern Asia. Indian rhinos have thick, bumpy skin with folds covering their bodies. Their skin looks and acts like armor! Indian rhinos are also known for the horns that grow above their noses. Each Indian rhino has only one horn, unlike some other types of rhinos that have two horns.

There are many different kinds of rhinos. This white rhino has two horns. White rhinos live in Africa.

Indian rhinos, like the one shown here, have one horn. This Indian Rhino lives in Nepal.

Indian rhinos are closely related to other rhinos, such as the Javan rhino, the Sumatran rhino, and the black rhino. Indian rhinos are the second-largest **species** of rhinos. Only white rhinos are larger. Indian rhinos are also related to tapirs.

Indian rhinoceroses once lived throughout the northern Indian **subcontinent**. This includes parts of present-day northern India, Pakistan, Nepal, Bhutan, and Bangladesh. They also may have lived in Myanmar and southern China. Today, there are less than 3,000 Indian rhinos left in the wild. They live mostly in national parks and nature **preserves** in northern India and Nepal.

Most Indian rhinos live in national parks. Kaziranga National Park in India is home to many Indian rhinos, such as this one.

Indian rhinos like to wallow, or roll around, in mud. This keeps them cool and also helps to keep away biting insects.

Indian rhinos like to live in grassy wetlands, swamps, and forests near rivers. These **habitats** have many places for rhinos to **wallow** and keep their bodies cool with water and mud. They also have lots of grass and other plants for Indian rhinos to eat.

Indian rhinos have brownish-gray skin with folds. Their skin is more than 1.5 inches (3.8 cm) thick in most places but thinner between the folds. Each adult Indian rhino has a horn above its nose. These horns can grow to be about 3 feet (1 m) long but are generally about 1 foot (.3 m) long. Indian rhinos' horns can grow back if they are broken off.

Indian rhinos have good hearing and a strong sense of smell. They are nearsighted, though. This means they can only see things that are close to them.

Indian rhinos are big, strong, and fast. Don't get in their way!

Adult Indian rhinos are generally about 6 feet (1.8 m) tall and 12 feet (3.6 m) long. They can weigh 4,800 to 6,600 pounds (2,177–2,994 kg). Although they are very big, Indian rhinos are fast runners. They can run up to 30 miles per hour (48 km/h).

Indian rhinos are mostly solitary animals. This means they spend most of their time alone. Male rhinos each have their own **territory**. Sometimes male rhinos fight with other males that come into their territory. They do not fight with their horns, though. Instead, they bite each other with their long, sharp lower teeth. Female rhinos come and go between territories.

Indian rhinos like to spend time in the water. It is very warm where they live, and the water helps to keep them cool.

Indian rhinos are most active at night and in the early morning. This is when they **graze** for food. During the daytime, they rest and wallow in nearby swamps, rivers, lakes, or ponds. Sometimes a group of rhinos may wallow together and then separate afterward.

Indian Rhino Facts!

1. Indian rhinos' horns are made of keratin. This is the same material that makes up human fingernails and animal hooves.

2. Indian rhinos eat 1 percent of their body weight each day. This means that a rhino that weighs 5,000 pounds (2,268 kg) can eat about 50 pounds (22.6 kg) of plants in a single day!

3. Indian rhinos are mostly hairless. The only hair on their bodies can be found at the tip of their tails and around their ears. They also have eyelashes.

4. Indian rhinos rub their horns against large rocks and trees to keep them from growing too long. This is like how humans clip their fingernails to keep them short!

5. Indian rhinos have thick pads on the bottoms of their feet. The pads act as pillows for their very heavy weight.

6. Indian rhinos can make many different noises, such as snorts and whistles. They often make noises to **communicate** with each other.

7. Indian rhinos often have birds riding on their backs. These birds help the rhinos by eating some of the insects that bite them.

8. Some zoos sell paintings made by Indian rhinos. A person helps the rhino by holding up a piece of paper, then the rhino uses its top lip as a paint brush!

Male and female Indian rhinos can **mate** at any time during the year. The female rhino will have a baby, or calf, about 16 months later. They are generally born between February and April. However, female rhinos have calves only about once every three years.

Calves do not have horns right away, but they do have thick skin and folds.

Indian rhino calves are born without horns. They weigh about 100 pounds (45 kg) when they are born. Calves stay with their mothers for their first two years. They drink their mothers' milk. When they are 3 to 5 months old, they also start eating plants. Calves' horns grow in when they are about one year old. Wild Indian rhinos can live to be about 40 years old.

Mothers and calves stick together until the calf is old enough to go out on its own.

Grazing and Grasping

Indian rhinoceroses are herbivores. This means they eat only plants. Indian rhinos eat mostly different kinds of grass. However, they also eat twigs, leaves, fruit, and plants that grow in water. Indian rhinos that live near farmland sometimes eat crops, such as rice, corn, and wheat.

Indian rhinos are big and tough, but they eat mostly grass.

This Indian rhino is eating grass in Kaziranga National Park.

Indian rhinos graze for food at night or early in the morning. They use their pointed upper lip to grasp onto grass and other plants. They may also use their horn to poke around for food. If there is a lot of grass to eat, sometimes a few rhinos will graze in a field close to one another.

Dangers of the Wild

Adult Indian rhinos have no animal **predators**. They are too big for predators in their habitat to kill. However, tigers hunt Indian rhino calves. Young rhinos are much smaller than adults and easier to catch. Male Indian rhinos also sometimes die after a fight with another male rhino.

Male Indian rhinos can hurt each other when they fight. This Indian rhino has a cut above his horn.

Indian rhino calves are much more vulnerable to predators, such as tigers, than adults.

After fighting, male rhinos may have lots of cuts and bites on their bodies. If these cuts or bites get **infected**, the rhino can die.

Even though they have thick skin, Indian rhinos can also be bitten by **parasites**, such as small insects, ticks, or leeches. These parasites can give rhinos **diseases** that may make them sick and die.

Indian rhinos were common animals in northern India, Nepal, and Pakistan until about 1600. However, between 1600 and 1900, wild Indian rhinos became in danger of dying out because of hunting. One reason people were hunting rhinos was to sell their horns. By 1900, there were only about 200 Indian rhinos left in the world.

After 1900, the governments of India and Nepal decided to protect Indian rhinos. They made it against the law to hunt rhinos. They also turned some of the places where rhinos and other wild animals live into wildlife preserves. However, **poachers** still sometimes hunt Indian rhinos for their horns.

All types of rhinos are hunted for their horns. Rhino horns are used in the traditional medicines of some Asian cultures. They are also used to make handles for daggers in some Middle Eastern countries.

21

Keeping Rhinos Safe

The number of wild Indian rhinos is slowly getting larger. Wildlife groups are working hard to keep rhinos safe from poachers. They also are working to keep rhino habitats safe from people who want to use the land for other things.

Today, 70 percent of the world's Indian rhinos live in India's Kaziranga National Park in Assam, India. Kaziranga National Park is a wildlife preserve that opened in 1905 to protect Indian rhinos. About 100 Indian rhinoceroses also live in zoos in the United States and around the world!

Glossary

communicate (kuh-MYOO-nih-kayt) To share facts or feelings.

diseases (dih-ZEEZ-ez) Illnesses or sicknesses.

graze (GRAYZ) To feed on grass.

habitats (HA-buh-tats) The surroundings where animals or plants naturally live.

infected (in-FEK-ted) Became sick from germs.

mate (MAYT) To join together to make babies.

native (NAY-tiv) Born or grown in a certain place or country.

parasites (PER-uh-syts) Living things that live in, on, or with other living things.

poachers (POH-cherz) People who illegally kills animals that are protected by the law.

predators (PREH-duh-terz) Animals that kill other animals for food.

preserves (prih-ZURVZ) Areas set aside for the protection of plants and animals.

species (SPEE-sheez) A single kind of living thing. All people are one species.

subcontinent (sub-KON-tin-ent) A landmass that is part of one of Earth's seven great landmasses.

territory (TER-uh-tor-ee) Land or space that is protected by an animal for its use.

wallow (WAH-loh) To roll around in mud or muddy water.

Index

Websites

Due to the changing nature of Internet links, PowerKids Press has developed an online list of websites related to the subject of this book. This site is updated regularly. Please use this link to access the list: www.powerkidslinks.com/aaa/rhino/